Recovery from Homelessness

by Patrick Gene Frank

patrickgfrank@gmail.com

ISBN-13: 9781535231732

ISBN-10: 1535231734

Independently published by:

Beckoning Dove Press, 15 Forest Lane, Arden, NC 28704

Acknowledgments

Thanks to family members, friends and professional helpers who helped me to advance from pre-homelessness through full recovery,

many kind souls who were supportive of my efforts along the way, and

Diana Ani Stokely,
for her artistic and editorial contribution.

Parts of the Forward: Homeless in Tennessee were published in the Knoxville News-Sentinel.

Table of Contents

Foreword: Homeless in Tennessee

On February 4, 2015, the Tennessee Legislature voted down Governor Haslam's humane proposal to expand health care coverage to low income residents who did not qualify for TennCare medical care coverage. It reminds me of the time I lived in Chattanooga, and how fortunate it was that I qualified for TennCare.

Prior to that time when I lived in Tennessee, I had been in Massachusetts and had become unemployed and homeless there. I now know that I had been struggling with undiagnosed Bipolar Disorder. I had been told at least twice that I may suffer from that mental illness, but I did not take it seriously. My life had descended into chaos: unable to maintain a stable living situation, struggled to find even a part-time job, wracked by impulsivity, poor decision making, mood swings, and broken marriages. All may have been symptoms of the disorder. Assisted by Health Care for the Homeless program, I began the process of mental health recovery. While continuing to live in a rehab shelter, I gradually began to get back on my feet. I was able to work again, and eventually held down two jobs.

That was when I decided to move back to the South, where I had grown up. At first, I lived with members of my extended family in Chattanooga. It was a source of pride to make my healthcare co-pays, and to pay my relatives some kind of rent to live with them. Eventually, I rented an apartment below Lookout Mountain for the summer, and in 1999, I managed to qualify for TennCare medical care coverage. It was a godsend to me, enabling me to continue the psychotropic medication regime, as well as make steps in recovery of the Bipolar Disorder. TennCare provided me with the means to recover my mental health, and that led to my becoming a contributing member of society once again.

After three years of recovery, I achieved a personal goal: a full-time job! I would be counseling Native American kids on a reservation in New Mexico, and, while on the reservation, I would continue to receive medical care through the Indian Health Service.

Now I live in the Blue Ridge area of North Carolina, have been happily married for more than a decade to my wife, an artist-crafter. Each summer we cross the border to the adjoining Tennessee mountains to participate in craft fairs.

Besides writing prose and poetry, I am a songwriter. I have been inspired to write a song to acknowledge the time I spent in Tennessee, and to show my appreciation for the hospitality that was shown to me there.

Proud to Call Tennessee My Home

A place where I don't ever feel alone,
Strangers seem to understand
The hunger of a rootless man,
Proud to call Tennessee my home.

Glad that here I chose to take my stand,
Folks are not afraid to shake my hand,
Glad to see the red sun rise
Upon this precious land and sky,
Proud to call Tennessee my home.

A man forever wandering is blessed
To find a place of peacefulness and rest,
A place to watch a great bird soar,
A mountain that I can explore,
Proud to call Tennessee my home.

A place where I can dream again and plan,
Day by day a harder working man,
A simple life, a quiet need,
A place to love, to plant a seed,
Proud to call Tennessee my home.

Regarding the current debate for extended health care benefits for low income residents, I urge you to consider: When low-income folks have access to good health care, many are enabled to give more back to their community. Governor Haslam is on the right track with his Insure Tennessee Plan.

As a diehard University of Tennessee fan, I must add: Go Volunteers!

Patrick Frank
Arden, North Carolina
February, 2015

Part I: Recognizing the Problem

Homelessness remains a major problem in America. Housing and Urban Development statistics showed that on any given day in 2012, more than 633,000 people were classified as homeless. In 2013, 1 child in 30 is homeless. It is ironic that, according to Amnesty International USA, vacant houses outnumber homeless people by five times.

The factors which may contribute to homelessness include job loss or job instability, low wages, marital breakdown, family dysfunction, substance abuse/or dependence, and various forms of discrimination and abuse. Government statistics indicate that 20-25% of the homeless population in the United States are afflicted with some form of major mental illness. Untreated mental illness is not the only factor leading to homelessness in America.

My own struggle with Bipolar Disorder undoubtedly contributed to my slide into homelessness. A major mental illness can cause impulsivity, poor judgment, mood swings, and lack of mental clarity. Ironically, for those who experience untreated mental disorders, homelessness can serve as a wake-up call. During the homeless and post-homeless periods, it is common to see a surge in deep and personal growth.

Within the United States, homeless face prejudice and rejection by others. They are viewed as lazy, takers (as opposed to givers), and/or self-willed alcoholics or drug addicts. Statistics reported by the National Coalition for the Homeless in 2009 indicate that between 30-40% of homeless individuals have struggled with drug/alcohol abuse or dependence; but it is also true that problems with substances can result from the severe stress of the homeless lifestyle, rather than vice versa. Further, it is likely that homeless individuals who lack access to ongoing psychiatric care have utilized drugs and/or alcohol as a form of self-medication. Finally, substance dependence transcends the notion that lack of will power prevents the alcoholic or drug addict from achieving abstinence and recovery. Once physical dependence is established, medical intervention and rehabilitation are frequently required to help the alcoholic or addict break the cycle of compulsive drinking or using.

A disturbing trend in the United States is for the homeless to be driven out of a growing number of communities, cities, and towns. Loitering laws, widespread use of public seating designed to prevent individuals from lying down, efforts to discourage churches and other organizations from providing free meals, and other measures attempt to eliminate the homeless problem by forcing it to go away, to move to another locality.

The pre-homeless period deserves closer study, as it lays the groundwork, in very stark terms, for the subsequent complete loss of independence. Believe it or not, it is sometimes difficult to tell if one is actually homeless, and that goes both for the individual and for outside observers. If stronger intervention were applied during the pre-homeless period, actual homelessness — a much deeper hole to climb out of — could be avoided.

Additionally, the post-homeless period requires study and planning, if only to avoid a relapse.

Part II: Introduction to Recovery

Within this book you will find ideas and strategies to help homeless individuals in their recovery of independence, self-esteem, and hope for the future. Additionally, I include some constructive approaches for dealing with helpers such as paid staff, volunteers, or significant others, with the goal to enhance their ability to make a difference in the lives of those in need.

This is no academic work replete with statistics, though relevant data on homelessness in America deserves mention.

My perspective on homelessness is primarily based on my residence in four shelters in Western Massachusetts. It was only a short period of time when I lived "on the street," because I was able to gain admission in a residential setting quickly, and therefore, have less personal familiarity with that aspect. There are many who have spent months or years on the street or have set up camp in the woods, and their experiences vary from mine.

Though not an autobiography, I include aspects of my own experiences here, using poetry, prose-poetry and song lyrics which were written during my own struggles with homelessness.

In this writing, I identify "pre-homelessness" and "homelessness," as both periods are fraught with trauma and worthy of our understanding. This book was written out of concern to help pre-homeless and homeless individuals to comprehend what they are going through and to gain insight into ways of extricating themselves as quickly as possible from the decline of their quality of life.

Part III: Identifying Pre-Homelessness

One of U2's seminal song lyrics speaks of homelessness, and upon hearing it, the words immediately resonated with me. My own experience with homelessness was preceded by a long period of deterioration, when I gradually lost my ability to hold a job, maintain relationships, budget money, drive safely, solve problems, retain emotional stability, reestablish impulse control, think ahead, etc. That, along with the progression of my untreated Bipolar Disorder, meant that I could no longer maintain an independent living situation.

Many homeless individuals have experienced that long period of deterioration. It seems more likely to happen if they have suffered from alcohol or drug addiction and other forms of mental illness. This formulation could apply to individuals who manifest personality disorders like sociopathy and narcissism. Frequently, narcissists and sociopaths alienate enough people to effectively ruin any supportive relationships and steady job prospects.

This long slow decay can sometimes lead to experiencing unremitting rejection and abuse. The resulting emotional and behavioral damage can get to the point where one is unable to maintain an independent existence in the community.

Pre-homelessness can last for years, even decades. The signs of deterioration may be hard to discern. Over time, one's inability to handle money responsibility can plunge the individual into such overwhelming debt that it may seem impossible to crawl out of the financial hole. The gradual inability to establish and maintain lasting relationships can result in what appears to be a life of permanent isolation. One's friendship network can diminish over time. A person who cannot hold onto a decent job can eventually develop such a crazy quilt resume -- not to mention a lack of good references -- that it becomes extremely difficult to gain another position which pays enough to cover rent, utilities, and the other routine expenses of viable independent living.

I urge those whose lifeway is simultaneously deteriorating in a number of respects, to make a concerted effort to interrupt the slide by, first, eliminating personal denial of the slide, and secondly, by acknowledging the pattern to a significant other who you feel has your best interests at heart. Typically, it will then prove necessary to seek effective counseling, therapy, psychiatry and/or treatment for substance dependence. Through such concerted actions, I believe that the descent into the abyss of long-term homelessness can be averted.

Most people understand that it is infinitely better to deal with a life problem or health problem early on. It can be very hard to accept that one has a major mental abnormality, or that one is alcohol or drug dependent.

I had to "hit bottom," i.e. become literally homeless, before I was ready to accept my mental health issues and pursue treatment. Perhaps for many individuals, hitting bottom is the only thing that will induce real personal change. The downward slide CAN be interrupted. Before more serious damage is done in your own life (and perhaps in the lives of those near you), I hope that by sharing these observations, discussing these issues, and keeping a journal, you will be encouraged to face your own troubles and to seek help along the way to recovery from homelessness.

Part IV: Challenges of Homelessness

When reading this book, journaling and discussion are encouraged. I share many thoughts designed to help homeless individuals come to grips with their own problems, beyond the help that may or may not be available to them in the community and from professional helpers.

This section is devoted to particular challenges inherent within the realm of homelessness. Opportunities to deal with them are provided with prompts relating to recovery, ongoing study, or reflection.

We Are All Homeless, In a Sense

You must come to realize that a stable life style is needed in order to function normally in our society, and that residential, occupational, relational, geographical stability does not mean a loss of creativity or "selling out" to corruption and selfishness in our cultural milieu.

Do you have a conflict between desiring to seek stability and a sense of freedom in your life?

Where does our sense of inner security come from?

Well, it has to come from inside, from the deepest part of the self, which, in my view, is connected with the farthest reaches of the universe. Now, we connect with that deep part of the self in various ways: through prayer or meditation, creative work and play, music or nature. But it's up to us to open our eyes to these possibilities. No one can do this inner work for us. No "guru" is going to make it happen.

How do you go about connecting with the deepest part of yourself?

The Loss of a Primary Relationship ...

can lead to general instability, a more transitory existence, wandering, the experience of feeling alienated from others, and eventually a kind of a numbed-out trauma feeling that can inhibit rational thought. The breakup of a relationship can have a great deal to do with job instability or working for inadequately low pay, which bothers the partner, and leads to friction. The job-pay situation may very well be related to the economy and political decision-making in DC, but there is little that you can do about that right now. Your primary focus is survival, not protest and that is understandable. How have primary relationship problems factored into your becoming homeless?

Job Loss Leading to Homelessness

Beyond the effect on primary relationships, the loss of a job remains a key factor leading to homelessness. It is not only the loss of income that comes into play. The loss of self-esteem that accompanies job-loss contributes to the spiraling effect that can result in a person finding him or herself sleeping in a shelter one day. Multiple job losses, of course, are even more devastating. Job loss, especially repeated job loss, for whatever reason, can lend to one's demeanor a quality of desperation that can be easy to pick up by an interviewer or recruiter. In addition, being desperate to get a job can lead one to take any offer that comes down the pike, no matter how inappropriate or doomed to failure.

Describe your job history? Has it contributed to your movement into homelessness?

But a Job Can Be the Kiss
of Death ...

if it is the wrong job in the wrong place and at the wrong time. Sometimes it is best to say no to a job even though you feel compelled by social or internal factors to say yes. Money, alone, cannot determine the decision to take a job or not. I took a couple of low-paying jobs during the period when I was climbing out of homelessness that turned out to be just right for me at the time—one, washing dishes part-time at a steakhouse, which provided some cash left me time to consider my next series of moves.

Have you taken a job that you feel did you more harm than good? Explain what happened.

Starting to Feel Human Again

Sometimes I say to my wife, "I'm starting to feel human. I'm starting to feel like myself." What does that exactly mean? And how does it relate to the homeless experience? When I say feeling human, etc., I mean what they refer to as "feeling comfortable in your own skin," as well as feeling comfortable in your surroundings. The fact is that it IS hard to feel comfortable in your own skin when you are wandering in what seems to be alien territory, like the inner city or, for that matter, the middle of nowhere.

In order to feel "human" and connected to the human race, I think that we must also feel that inner connection with ourselves; the two go hand in hand. What this means is that one is experiencing a kind of flow, a life force that emanates from within and from beyond at the same time. Weighed down by alienation, it is hard to feel that life force.

Do you feel that sense of humanity and connection to the human race?

Rebuilding One's Life, a Complex Project

To rebuild one's life while homeless or after homelessness is a complex process that is a form of work in itself. Those of us who have been there, or are there, must accept that fact, and make plans accordingly. A great deal of simple patience and common sense are required to get back on one's feet; moving back to an independent status does not happen overnight, and that's an understatement.

Are you feeling impatient about the length of time it is taking you to move out of homelessness?

The Primacy of Hope

As long as you retain a sense of hope for positive change, you're still okay, though you may be sleeping in an army cot in a rundown shelter.

Are you feeling that sense of hope? Why or why not?

So Much Depends on Courage

The fact is that creativity and other key coping skills need not vanish as one ages, especially if nutritional needs are met. The aging person must recognize that he or she need not succumb to the stereotype of the aging person as mentally deficient, or even incompetent. So much depends on courage, the ability to fight back, and finally, the willingness to shed denial and seek competent professional help.

What do you think courage has to do with your recovery process as a homeless individual?

Respect the Public Library

It is important not to abuse the privilege of using a public library—like hogging the free access, surfing porn sites, wasting time playing computer games. I would focus on communicating with family and friends, creative writing, and looking for jobs or housing. To defeat the stereotype of homeless people as irresponsible, act responsibly!

Have you used the public library to advance your recovery? Why or why not?

Sharing Writing with Others

Creative writing can be shared with others, or not. I find it is more helpful if I do share it with others in some way. It deepens one's connection to others, for one thing, if you share thoughts and feelings in this way.

How do you feel about sharing your writing with others? Have you done so in the past?

Make Your Music

Music can also be a great outlet. If you should happen to still own your guitar, you can play or even make up a number of new songs. I wrote a number related to homelessness that I would sometimes share on the guitar. Listening to positive or thoughtful music, also, can lead to spiritual growth.

Do you enjoy singing or playing an instrument? What are your favorite songs? How does music help you to relax or grow as a person?

Writing: Both Work and Play

It's not really such a big deal, being a writer, though society tends to think so. It is work and play at the same time, but need not separate you from the human race. It's just an ability or genetic disposition that may have come to the fore in the midst of crisis. Keep on writing, keep on playing. Don't allow the creative spirit to die.

In your past experience, has writing felt like work or play? What about now? Talk or write about this.

Family May Understand,
or Not

Family may or may not understand why you might be homeless. Many will not reach out to help, but a few will. Some may be secretly glad that it is you who have hit bottom and not them. Someone in the family to gossip about or feel superior to has surfaced. Many people have serious problems of their own that they want to keep hidden, and someone else's flameout takes the focus off their own problems. Don't worry about it. If just one family members accepts you, understands, and believes in your potential to grow, that is enough.

How has your family reacted to your homelessness?

Timing Is Everything

Some family members may come up with unrealistic ideas about how to extricate oneself from homelessness. There are the "pull yourself up by your bootstraps" jokers. Someone may offer you a place to stay, but it may not be the right time for that, and may not be a good idea anyway. Timing is everything. I reached a point in my recovery where I realized that I needed to pursue recovery, basically, outside of the orbit of family. At a later point, I did live with extended family, while I continued with my long-term recovery process.

Again, timing is everything.

Recovery Does Not Happen Overnight

In most cases, you didn't get to homelessness overnight, and won't be able to extricate yourself from the situation overnight, as well. There are usually complicated factors that lead one into the street or a shelter that will have to be unraveled.

You may need mental health or substance abuse treatment. You may, in effect, have to learn to work again after an extended period of sporadic employment, or no employment. You may have to make important decisions about where to live and when to move — when it is appropriate to make a geographical move.

There Is a Time to Move and a Time to Stay Put

Some people regard any tactic that smacks of a "geographical cure" as wrongheaded, but hanging on in an environment that is sapping your spirit may be the strategy that is wrongheaded. For me, it was necessary to move from Southern New England back to the South for a variety of reasons, but I had to make that move back at the right time.

You, as a homeless person, might want to move immediately away from your immediate environment, but have to save sufficient money to make a successful move; it takes some planning and some degree of financial sense.

The ability to handle finances may be a big part of your problem that needs to be worked on before you make a major move.

You Must Emerge from the Cocoon Sometime

You may become comfortable in a protected setting like a rehab shelter or program and simply not want to face the unknown of continuing the recovery process on your own. This is a natural feeling, not something to be ashamed of. Someone might have to give you a nudge to move on from such a protected setting, and sometimes more than a nudge.

Re-Learning to Care
About Others

Self-confidence and self-regard are rebuilt gradually through a series of responsible activities. You gradually learn to be genuinely concerned about the fate of others; over time you become less self-involved and you get to the point where a prime goal for you is to become a contributing member of society once again.

Seek Good Mental and Physical Care

Pre-homelessness or homelessness present dangers and damage to body and mind that might prove irreversible. For those folks whose lives seem to be headed in the direction I am describing, I recommend that you seek mental and physical intervention early in the period of decline. You might have to do some heavy searching for competent help. Not every professional whom you approach is necessarily equipped to respond effectively to the problems you present.

Be smart about choosing a person to confide in and seek advice from. Examine credentials, but also trust your gut. Having a prestigious degree is not equivalent to having wisdom. I value wisdom in a helper, above all.

Homelessness Is a Red Flag

The truth is that many people go through significant ups and down in life, so you are not alone. But pre-homelessness and homelessness are red flags indicating the need for a strong focus on opening up to others and getting help.

Help Yourself First, Then Help Others

If you are struggling with your own issues, don't get lost in helping others, tapping your own resources to the point where you are thrown off-center. Give what you can, emotionally, in terms of what you know, and time-wise, and then let it go.

If you have been helpful, the person will return to you and if he/she has made significant gains, offer sincere thanks.

Avoid Blaming "The System" or Others

Political ranting, blaming your fate on "the system," is also not helpful. We all know that social, cultural, and political factors play a significant part in facilitating the growth of the homeless population in America. But obsessing about these factors or playing the victim role will be counterproductive in your own recovery. That's my view, anyway. Others may urge the homeless to engage in activism. I think that is a mistake until you are back on your feet.

It is self-defeating to get in the habit of blaming other individuals — parents, spouses, friends, employers, the police, etc. Yes, you may have been treated terribly, but now your job is to focus on your part of the equation that led you to actual homelessness. We can't control others, but we can control our reaction to people and events that occur.

When You Do Attempt to Help Others...

It is important that in reaching out to others, that the homeless person be diligent in not crossing boundaries. Simply satisfying personal needs for companionship, romance, or sex, or as an access to housing, a job, or money, is self-defeating and defeats the purpose of the act.

Give a Smile

A smile in the midst of travail, it can simply lift the spirit at a time when spirit is on the verge of being obliterated. That's all there is to it. No words required in that moment.

Give a smile. It will come back to you.

Chart Your Own Pathway
to Recovery

No one can tell you exactly what you are doing right or wrong, when you are in the midst of homelessness. People might make well-meaning or not so well-meaning suggestions, and do pay heed to them, but ultimately, you must chart your own pathway back to independent living and a sense of well-being.

When it feels like someone is leading you down a path that they have chosen for you, this can strip you of the pride you might otherwise feel if you have taken the initiative yourself to chart the course and move forward.

A "Normal" Existence Can
Feel Strange

When you start to move out of homelessness, it can simply feel strange to adopt a "normal" lifestyle, not to mention the challenges of cleaning your own living space (usually a room or efficiency), figuring out what to do with your extra belongings, doing laundry (probably at a coin laundry), getting your car running again and legal, getting to a job (usually fairly menial) and performing adequately, getting used to living alone if you have been living in a shelter or rehab shelter.

A Shelter or Long-Term Rehab
Can Become Too Comfortable

Some formerly homeless folks might feel drawn back into the shelter environment, because it is simply familiar. You may have formed a relationship with a staff person or homeless resident whom you greatly miss. It might even be tempting to allow your non-homeless life to disintegrate; it is possible, unconsciously, to seek failure so that you can return to the shelter.

Find a Creative Outlet

I think that if the homeless person can engage in some form of creative expression, whether it be writing a poem, keeping a journal, painting a picture or playing a song, etc., this kind of activity can be of enormous benefit — both emotionally and spiritually.

Thankfully, I was able to continue with my creative writing, music-making and journaling during my pre-homeless, homeless, and post-homeless periods.

Facilities Should Encourage
Creative Expression

It would be good for shelters and homeless rehab centers to find a way to encourage creative expression; a simple open-mic could be established for homeless individuals; it could also be open to outside participation. In this way, the homeless person could perhaps become integrated with a creative community outside of the facility.

Interaction that is restricted to other homeless people and staff certainly can inhibit growth and confidence in one's ability to reestablish residential independence and involvement in the wider community.

Dealing with Guilt and Remorse

Usually, before we become homeless, we have made a number of mistakes in life that may have caused pain to others. Forgiving ourselves can be very difficult. But being weighed down with guilt can steal energy from our recovery process in the present. Sometimes talking to pastor can help, other times a counselor or therapist can help. Sometimes it is best to make amends to the person we have hurt. Sometimes a simple and sincere apology can make a big difference. Other times trying to make amends with someone from the pain can cause more pain than it is worth.

If you are so inclined, sometimes simple and sincere prayer can make a huge difference.

Dealing with Arrogant People

You will encounter arrogant people along the way during your journey into (and hopefully) out of homelessness. Arrogant staff, arrogant homeless folks, arrogant strangers. There is a significant amount of arrogance in our culture. And you, too, will probably be subject to arrogance in the way you interact with others.

Arrogance often produces either an angry or a fearful response from others. If you encounter someone who is behaving in an overbearing, self-righteous and critical manner in relating to you, try not to overreact in response. Realize that the problem is with the arrogant person, not you. Stand up for yourself but avoid getting involved in a shouting match. See if you can express your point of view forthrightly, but calmly, then walk away.

Don't allow your day to be ruined by an arrogant person.

Hold Off on Intense Involvement

While in the midst of homelessness, I did avoid romantic relationships. When you are homeless you are in crisis. There may be a tendency to jump into an intense relationship — as a way to avoid dealing with one's own serious life problems. It may feel good at the time, but intense involvement is likely to add to one's stress quotient. I would suggest holding off on romance until you have achieved emotional, residential, and job stability once again. At that point you will have much more to offer to a love. Address your personal problems first, then you will naturally be much more capable of engaging in an equal, give-and-take relationship.

That's my advice, though no one can dictate who is going to fall in love with whom, and when this is apt to occur.

Avoid Co-Dependence

Maintain healthy boundaries with others — avoid co-dependence. Each homeless person is well advised to avoid leaning on others so much that you become a pain, while losing the ability to cope independently with your own problems.

Friendships are fine, but a friendship in which over-dependency is encouraged quickly devolves into something less than friendship,

Be Selective in Your
Deep Sharing

You don't have to reveal your heart and soul to every person who crosses your path. Save the deep sharing for your therapist, counselor, doctor, confidential support group, or a special friend, or, if you are lucky, a handful of friends.

Seek Immediate Help When You Have Lost Hope

When you feel that you have lost hope for positive change in your life is, of course, a serious warning sign. You need to talk to a trusted person about such feelings. Hope is a crucial precursor of recovery. Also, gather people around you who convey a positive attitude, who instill in you the feeling that they genuinely believe that you can effect significant positive change in your life.

Loss of hope, if it becomes a long-term and very entrenched phenomenon, is a symptom of serious depression; if you feel you are trapped in the feeling that you have no hope, run, don't walk to a facility where you can receive psychiatric or psychological help or at least a good referral. Find a professional who takes your plight seriously and sets aside adequate time to address it.

Stand Up to Unresponsive Bureaucracy

Do not permit yourself to be bullied by an impersonal bureaucracy. Stand up for yourself if you feel you are being treated like a number rather than a person while your real needs are being ignored. But do not have a temper tantrum in the process. As calmly as possible, convey your frustration with the "bureaucrat," who might be just as frustrated with the system as you are.

Seek concrete answers to your questions.

Write things down.

Help the bureaucracy to help you.

Don't give up.

Keep a Daily To-Do List

Keeping a to-do list on daily basis can play a vital role in giving the homeless person a sense of direction during what may seem like an interminable period of transition out of homelessness. You can divide the list into sections: Creative objectives, Relationship objectives, Work objectives, Health objectives, and Business objectives, for example.

That's how I did it, anyway and continue with that format even today. When you achieve an objective for the day, just cross it off your list.

Some of your objectives listed may actually be longer term goals, but that's fine. It's good to keep in mind the longer term goals.

And don't worry about the ones that you are unable to achieve. Rome wasn't built in a day, to borrow the cliché.

Avoid Falling Back Into
the Rat-Race

You may feel that when you become homeless that you have finally escaped from the rat race of ordinary life in America — driving too fast, long commutes, working overtime, incessant worry over bills to pay and bills unpaid, the unseen pressure to "keep up with the Joneses," etc. What a relief. But don't make the mistake of relaxing too much in homelessness. You will have to return to the life of full-time work, taking care of personal business, family responsibilities and the like eventually.

A moderate amount of life stress is to be expected in today's world, But take care not to fall back into a pattern of working all the time, worrying all the time, racing around recklessly, etc. Such a pattern can lead you right back into homelessness when you become emotionally and physically exhausted once again and that manic pattern continues for a considerable period of time.

Deal with Details While
Seeing the Big Picture

It is important to deal effectively with the details of life — in and outside of homelessness, while simultaneously keeping your eye on the big picture: your life as a whole, past, present and future. While your goal should NOT be to rush out of homelessness prematurely, a return to the mainstream of life in America, to an independent and productive way of life, is certainty a worthy goal to shoot for. It might take you six months, a year or more to get to the point where you are ready to move out of a shelter and resume full-time work.

Good transition goals are to work part-time while saving money for a car and/or rental deposit, along with last month's rent, etc.

The details are important, but so is the big picture.

Seek Justice for Self
AND Others

Never prey on others or use them in a selfish way. Life is about give and take. Don't be a taker, a fast talker, a manipulator. Keep in the forefront of your mind the other person's needs, not simply your own.

One of my favorite sayings is this: Seek justice not only for yourself, but for others, as well.

People may have seen you as a user and manipulator in the past, but you can change their image of you and that pattern. It may take time, but people in your former life should notice the difference eventually.

And if they refuse to abandon that old negative image of you, after a significant amount of time has passed, then the problem lies within them, not you. This problem can be termed "a fixed, judgmental attitude."

Don't Worry About Rejection, Make New Friends

Don't worry about those who reject you. You can (and will) make new friends after returning to a responsible life pattern. And not everyone from the past is likely to reject you. Making new friends can be tremendously exciting, because new friends can bring out positive aspects of your personality that you did not even know existed. Making new friends can induce a creative response in you.

When people see you in a new light and like what they see, this can be a tremendously exhilarating experience.

Nothing Wrong with Having "Just" One or Two Friends

There is nothing wrong with just having one or two friends. That may be the normal course of events for most people. Some people have many friends, but the communication between you and them may be relatively superficial. So your goal need not be to collect friend after friend, online or offline.

The Upside and Downside of Online Social Networking

Nowadays, many homeless folks ARE utilizing social networking, at least through a public access computer. As with most things in life, there can be an up-side and down-side to social networking. While it is possible to make genuine friends online, there are many scammers and superficial people out there who you should not waste your time on.

Google and other search engines can serve a valuable research function, of course, helping the homeless person to explore job and educational opportunities, as well as medical resources, good banks, spiritual communities, places to worship, 12-step meetings and the like. But overuse of the computer can certainly separate one from flesh-and-blood involvement with people and constructive engagement with the concrete, immediate world.

Maintaining Your Personal Hygiene

When homeless, it is vitally important to maintain personal hygiene and physical health as best you can. There are a multitude of "bad germs" floating around in any homeless shelter. Shower regularly. Wash your clothes at a shelter, or at a coin laundry, if you can afford it. Homeless folks are frequently exposed to extreme outdoor temperatures and weather conditions. Such exposure, especially if repeated, presents challenges to the maintenance of one's physical and mental well-being.

Homeless folks may be subject to Emergency Room visits, where quality medical care may be in short supply and a variety of noxious germs may be plentiful. Make a strong effort to take daily multivitamins and to eat a balanced diet. Soup kitchens and food banks can be a godsend in that regard. Avoid excessive alcohol consumption. If you are addicted to drugs or alcohol, get professional help and check out the 12-step programs.

Finally, self-esteem is enormously enhanced when you are clean, neat and healthy in body and mind.

Get Help for Mental Illness or Addiction

If you know you have a major mental illness, or suspect this is the case, do your best to obtain competent professional help. Those who suffer from untreated Bipolar, Schizophrenia, Major Depression and the like are likely to deteriorate rapidly when subjected to homelessness. Mental illness is not something to be ashamed of. But those who fail to seek out or accept treatment are sabotaging their own chance for recovery of independent living and positive self-esteem.

Part V: Helping the Homeless

It is understandable that some homeless folks would want to reach out to each other and offer some kind of help. It is also understandable that other homeless folks may want to hold back and focus on their own problems. It can be beneficial to strike a balance between helping and holding back when you feel the urge to reach out to a peer in the homeless situation. Sometimes, the best way to help peers is to be a healthy role model, displaying self-motivation, a sense of courage, responsibility, creativity, honesty, and hope for the future.

Occasionally, a seemingly magical relationship between homeless folks occurs when mutual and unselfish helpfulness is established. In other words, homeless folks can develop genuine, in-depth and long-lasting friendships. But I would put emphasis on the word "occasionally." Many times the homeless person is, understandably, concerned with straightening out his or her own life and moving on to independent living, improving their mental and physical health, finding work and developing relationships with folks who are not homeless.

Family Members Striving to
Help the Homeless

Family may or may not understand why you might be homeless. Many will not reach out to help, but a few will. Some may be secretly glad that it is you who have hit bottom and not them. Others may be glad to have a feeling of superiority over someone the family, keen to start the gossip. Many people have serious problems of their own that they want to keep hidden, and someone else's flameout takes the focus off their own problems.

Some may come up with unrealistic ideas about how to extricate oneself from homelessness. There are the "pull yourself up by your bootstraps" jokers. Someone may offer you a place to stay, but it may not be the right time for that, and may not be a good idea anyway. Timing is everything.

It may be a good thing for a newly homeless person to go through the tedious process of the beginning stage of recovery on his or her own. Maybe a person needs to engage in his or her own struggle back to independence in order to grow in some important way. It all depends. I did live with extended family members during one stage in the process of recovery, but if I had done so at the outset, I think it could have proved a disaster. I am very grateful to this couple — of course — but I had to know that I could initiate the recovery process on my own before taking the next step to recovery.

Some may, in effect, want to steal your accomplishment and cast themselves in the role of martyr or savior. Stay away from these rescuers.

There are family members who simply cannot comprehend what you are going through, others who do know, because they have been there or in a similar place. Some may offer a well-timed suggestion rather than deluging you with a series of directives — you must do this or that according to my sense of good timing. But a suggestion, lightly delivered, can be instrumental in moving you forward to the next stage of recovery.

Some family members panic when they find out you are homeless; others take it in stride and convey the fact that they have faith in you, in your ability to work yourself out of the situation.

It all depends. Some families are extremely dysfunctional and it would be good to keep your distance from them while you deal with the struggle out of homelessness. And it is usually a struggle.

Staff and Volunteers Helping the Homeless

Here is a list of do's and don'ts for paid and volunteer staff working with pre-homeless and homeless folks in shelters, drop-in centers, clinics, emergency rooms and the like. I will use the term "client" to refer to any pre-homeless or homeless individual we are striving to work with.

- Strive to manifest empathy, genuineness and unconditional positive regard in your work with these individuals. These three qualities were identified by Dr. Carl Rogers as vital facilitative ingredients — decades ago, and they remain relevant today, at least as ideals to strive for in working with clients, patients or anyone in need of emotional support or guidance.

- Don't make any promises you can't keep.

- Respect the diverse religious or spiritual beliefs of clients, or their right to not espouse religious or spiritual beliefs.

- Do not tolerate any physical or emotional abuse of a client — by a fellow client or staff member. Report clear misconduct in this regard.

- Maintain your boundaries with homeless clients. You are there to help, not to make a close personal friend or locate a romantic partner. Granted, this is one of the hardest guidelines to adhere to. Discuss any problem you are having, or have had, in this area with someone you trust. Get the issue out on the table.

- Be alert to signs of major depression. Take suicidal thoughts expressed by clients seriously. Make appropriate referrals immediately if you feel that the client is at risk, in terms of suicidality.

- Make appropriate medical, psychiatric, housing, job and financial assistance referrals.

- Do not tolerate drug or alcohol use in your facility.

- Discourage panhandling or any type of scamming behavior on the part of the homeless.

- Directly confront any serious issue with personal hygiene. Disease can spread easily in a homeless environment.

- Take care of yourself. Get plenty of R and R. Do not work so much that you put yourself at risk for a physical or emotional breakdown. You can't help anyone when you are in desperate need of help yourself.

- Avoid displaying a bureaucratic or detached attitude when working with homeless clients. Strive to not display coldness.

- Some clients you are going to like, others you will have a neutral attitude toward, and some you will clearly not like. Regardless of whether you like a client or not, each client deserves basic respect and the best care you can provide.

- If you screw up in some area, don't condemn yourself, sometimes they are justified. Talk guilt feeling over with someone. Realize that — despite our best efforts — not everyone can be helped by us at any given point in time. Plant a seed of insight. It may sprout long after we are no longer on the scene.

- Avoid a martyr complex. Working with the homeless can be perceived as extremely heroic work by others. Don't make the mistake of feeding your own ego on the exaggerated adulation of outside observers. You are not Dr. Freud. You are not God. Good work is good enough. You do not have to be God's gift to the helping community.

- One day at a time. One client at a time.

If you are a volunteer, you may find that unexpectedly a homeless person will come up to you and for some reason trust you enough to share a deep concern. There must be an instant connection made in his or her mind. This is a humbling and very gratifying experience at the same time. But you can't predict when this will happen. And it usually happens one to one, not in a group. When this happens, I try mainly to be a good listener and may offer, mildly, a suggestion or two. But mainly I try to display empathy and offer compassion.

Part VI: Post-Homelessness: Choppy Waters

Post-homelessness, the period which follows recovery from homelessness, is not all smooth sailing. The problems which led to homelessness in the first place are probably not completely resolved.

For instance, recovery from the effects of extended untreated mental illness can take a very long time. Some residual problems can continue for life.

My own experience post-homelessness had many positive notes. The multiple car accidents and tickets I had known before gradually faded away to nothing. My ability to maintain a positive intimate relationship improved, and my marriage has lasted more than a decade. My ability to maintain personal boundaries has also improved, and my creativity and productivity as a writer have blossomed.

Not all experiences were so pleasant. There were occasions of problematic manic episodes, which led to some inappropriate behavior, causing irritation for others, especially my wife.

Post-homelessness is far from problem-free. No one is completely "cured" of Bipolar, just as no one is completely "cured" of addictive tendencies. But overall, the problems should decrease in severity to the point where a "normal" lifestyle becomes very attainable.

Problems with personal relations should improve over time, but then you may find new concerns with finding or keeping a job. Why? I do not have a complete answer. If you, like me, have a history of multiple jobs, understand that it is a red flag. Perhaps the jobs offered post-homelessness generate too much high stress, or pay lower-than-average wages, setting up a situation for failure. Without that steady income, it could be difficult to pay the rent.

Simply adjusting to being on your own could be difficult. If you have been residing in a homeless shelter or rehab facility for months, simply being alone in a room or small apartment could induce depression. If you are living with family members during the post-homeless period, tensions may arise. The transitional problems could lead to the homeless individual returning to a homeless shelter or rehab facility.

I would advise post-homeless folks to participate in counseling, therapy or join a support group. I attended a support group while working at an alternative school in Toledo, Ohio. It consisted of folks in recovery from major mental illness. I also made sure I received regular medical care while staying on my psychotropic medication. Even now, I continue to see a psychiatrist and participate in therapy sessions every 3-4 weeks, or so.

I am now in my 70s and have a couple of significant physical problems, but my brain is sharp and my creativity is in high gear.

I am thankful that my wife, her family, and my adult son have loved me throughout it all.

I have taken my own steps to 'Help the Homeless.' I have written a column for the Knoxville News-Observer to focus on a program in the Smoky Mountain area of Eastern Tennessee which is designed to lead the homeless toward independence.

Additionally, for the past couple of years, I have organized open mic sessions in shelters and other facilities, which allow and encourage creative expression of the very poor/homeless speakers, writers, singers, and musicians.

Part VII: The Creativity of Homelessness

Creativity and self-affirmation serve as important tools of growth for the homeless individual. Facilities designed to help the homeless must encourage creativity of the homeless, and provide a venue for sharing that creative work.

Maybe you question if homeless individuals are capable of making music or engaging in creative writing. My response is: Many homeless folks have intelligence and creativity that is untapped, don't underestimate their contribution.

The following prose, poetry and song lyrics were written before, during, and after the time when I was homeless. Such a traumatic period generated intense feelings and deep thinking. Writing prose-poetry/poetry helped me to cope, while increasing my understanding of what I was going through. Call it a form of ventilation, if you will, but creative work does more than provide an outlet for emotions; I believe it also has the potential to enhance insight or deeper mindfulness.

After Moving Out of My
Girlfriend's House,

in the run-up to homelessness, I slept one night in a temporary shelter with army cots and ceiling fans in Springfield, Mass.

I became obsessed with a woman. Eventually, we got high. After she left me alone one night, I OD'd on a bottle of aspirin, then drove myself to an ER for help.

After they pumped my stomach, I told the crisis worker I was afraid of losing my grip on existence. She did not seem to hold out much hope that I could stop the downward slide.

(pre-homelessness)

One Time I Got Sick on a
State Street Bus and Hid

behind K-Mart, somewhere in a lot with barren trees and junk.

I played basketball beside Burger King, usually alone but sometimes with strangers. There were no nets. I remember gang signs, red and black, on a slatted wooden fence. Once my ex-girl visited me with her son in a rooming house where brown water fell from the ceiling, in a shower stall.

(pre-homelessness)

A Long Road Back, 1997 ...

I'm working as a counselor, living at a rooming house for the homeless, walking everywhere. Where is my car? I am separated from my woman, eating at the soup kitchen. How come I am homeless? I don't know how to rent my own place. How come? An Irish lady who runs the soup kitchen is the only one who knows me. I have no friends anywhere around.

I'm calling an 800 number on the pay phone outside the bus station, trying to get sex, but it does not work. I'm riding the bus back and forth to the rust belt town I hail from. One time I get sick on the bus and everyone makes fun of me. Now I remember I did have a car but wrecked it on the interstate. My room has a bed and a beat up dresser and chair. The bathroom is shared. One night, a cold night, the heat is not working so I turn on my hot plate, put it too near the bed, which catches fire to the bedclothes, which I throw on the roof. The firemen come to put out the blaze. I have a radio but the antenna is a pair of pliers. I wear tennis shoes to work, though I am a professional.

(pre-homelessness)

One Day I Risked Everything

to escape from living with strangers who wanted only my money. I was actually homeless but could not face it so I drove on the Mass. Pike with bald tires to apply for a job in Worcester. I remember plowing into a half-mile of yellow cones in slow motion, but escaping from the State Police because they were on the other side of the median.

I finally arrived at my interview for a counseling job. After fifteen minutes I could tell it was going bad.

The next thing I remember is driving down a steep hill, headed back to Ware, when suddenly my brakes completely failed. In the end, something deep inside made me drive off the road to wreck the car but save myself, and other travelers.

(pre-homelessness)

I Think I Was in My
Bipolar Haze

and homeless already when I drove to Cambridge in my rattletrap car and "crashed" with my son and his roommate in Ashdown House. I was separated from my third wife. We fantasized that a homeless man could live forever in the labyrinthine basement of Mike's dorm. He would have to sneak in and out to avoid detection.

I remember Mike and his roommate and I watching Star Trek and playing Maelstrom, warding off aliens on their Macintosh desktop. After they went to asleep, I would escape to the all-night coffee shop at the Student Union to read poetry and Scientific American and write in my journal. I must have looked strange in my retro outfit.

It was the end of winter. This was the season before I entered a real shelter back in Springfield and got help for my problem.

(in homelessness)

In the Lot of a Truck Stop
After Dark,

sleep eludes me. I am afraid and do not want to be seen, caught up in the whine of semis from the interstate, lost, with no future or escape. (In Homelessness)

In the donut shop, a man stares at me with angry eyes.

I remind him of someone from the past and he can tell I am now homeless, unshaven, wearing tattered jeans.

I am passing my mom's cemetery, but where is her grave? I am driving to the court where I shot hoop before.

I need help.

(in homelessness)

At Dusk, Riding the Bus

back to nowhere. At the diner I mingled with truckers. I find baseball cards on the shoulder of the highway. My tie is askew and my shoes are covered in mud. State police search the bags of this vagrant. I wonder when or if I will ever find a place to settle down.

(in homelessness)

After Quitting

one of my jobs, and separating from my third wife, I drove my rattle-trap car out to five-mile pond and swam beneath the brown water.

At some point, I lost my single room and came to live in my car. I slept in the parking lot of a truck stop beside the interstate for a few weeks. I remember light flickered on my windshield at two am, and not being able to sleep. My last night on the street, I parked under an overpass, not far from a tiny Catholic church. Darkness became blackness inside my mind.

Finally, at dawn, I called from a phone booth to a shelter where I could stay longer than one night. I remember driving back to the City of Springfield, to the Worthington Street Shelter. Later on, I made an appointment with Health Care for/ And my car began rusting into a piece of junk while I began to heal.

(transitioning from homelessness into a shelter environment)

Walking Up the Hill

from the shelter at seven a.m., headed to the donut shop where the locals hang out.

I don't remember what happened to my car. I had my gym bag, with stuff to read and write. The folks ignored me and talked about their own thing.   I wrote in my journal, searching within for a vision of hope, some semblance of a plan. I planned to walk to the bus station locker to check on my things.

(in homelessness)

Walking Past an
Abandoned Car

behind the shelter, knee-deep in weeds with no color of green, past Northampton State Hospital, now closed, with shattered glass, Ken, the addict, who will die soon, appears out of the mist.

I walk from the shelter on a road seldom used. There are weeds around here that are never cut down. I pass the old State Hospital. Some of its windows are broken out, and its walls are covered in graffiti. I imagine patients of the past, chained to their beds. I know some of them never had visitors or a shred of hope of escaping to the light.

I walk alone to the coffee shop, in winter. A car drives by and no one waves.

The weeds around here are chalk-white, yellow or brown.

I am Headed for the Café

where I read, write and dream of Tennessee, where I imagine a woman to love, country music, and a steady job.

I wish I could comfort the ghosts who are chained, the ones I must leave behind, when I ride a Trailways Bus sometime soon, back to the South.

The deepest green I cherish is visible to my mind.

(in homelessness)

Well Past Midnight

*Nontraditional haiku poetry,
depicting homeless, pre-homeless, and
post homeless experiences.*

birds suddenly take flight. spirit of a man lifted

calm spirit in the shelter ripples of peace expand

feeling my love fade away fade away

hard to face the truth I really am sick

head down standing in line a homeless man

heart empty no quarter to call my girl

homeless, alone but the snow falls gently

homeless man scared by his mirror image

homeless shelter my head is in my hands

some part of me has the desire to disappear

soup kitchen homeless woman feeds pigeons

the planets shining brighter, closer, closer

this time really locked in, really homeless

walking on the shoulder of the road, lost

walking, walking, walking alone, alone

at dusk riding the bus back to nowhere.

at the diner I mingle with truckers

I find baseball cards on the shoulder of the highway

my tie is askew and my shoes are covered in mud

my woman is far away dimly in mind

state police search the bags of this vagrant

when will he find a way to settle down

a big semi rushes past, blinding me

calming his spirit, the dark trees at dusk

cradling a wounded bird in his shirt

dawn. walking downtown. homeless, but at peace

eagle's silent flight, on a distant shore

father long gone. he loved the sea like me

finally, I used my one-way ticket back to the South

flashing in winter light, unseen below, silent wings

ghetto dog weakly rises when I pass

greeting other homeless and travelers

head down, standing in line, a homeless man

heart empty. No quarter to call my girl

homeless, alone, but the snow falls gently

in a storage bin, sorting through my life

in Motel 6, a woman parts much too soon

in spite of debt, there must be an answer

in the shelter, Ken plays his Irish music for me

I walk miles down the highway, my bag stuffed with poems

jailed kid alone. his grandfather dies

late winter snow. an old man's shot true in sunlight

making a space in my single room, and in my heart

light slowly fades at dusk. strumming guitar

man punished for admitting he needs help

miles distant woman in my life. let her be free

my body releasing last night, alone

my companion, a parolee, handcuffed

my old friend George Fair. goat behind his shack

no word from my girl and no job today

on the street, faint fluttering of a bird

parking on the street, I face the unknown

planet closer to a sliver of the moon

poet and dishwasher cross the railroad tracks at dawn

razor wire all over town. In prison and out

romantic song lifts the spirit of a rootless man

some part of me has the desire to disappear

spring dawn. bird's cry unceasing

standing in the mist, beside the empty road, a train

Things I Tell Myself

- I love poetry books that have a theme. They have an anchor, help the reader to figure out what the h___ is going on.

- Infinitely better to write a poem than to explain it. The latter is a boring exercise that fails to lift the soul.

- Inner consistency and random approaches to creativity both are vital.

- It is important to be forthright but very mindful in word and deed, to avoid causing harm to self or others.

- I value uniqueness but also the things that connect me to others.

- I want to go backwards and forward in time. Life is about making something special out of the ordinary.

- Listen to the silence and a message will begin to take shape.

- Listen to the voice of the crow: he has a message for you.

- Little things of life, together, they add up to something bigger--the fabric of one's life.

- Make your to-do list and then do it.

- Meditate daily on the changes you want to make.

- Memory can be a treasure-trove, pointing you in new directions. It need not be a cause for distress.

- Most people have a variety of ways of being in the world, and that's just fine.

- Never give up on your most cherished dreams.

- No matter what pain is burning inside, the writer continues to write.

- Pay attention to dreams but come up with your own interpretation.

- People who always are selling their art turn people off.

- Play others' music low so you can hear your own music.

- Perhaps we explore an alternate universe in dreams.

- Poetry, when it comes, is a gift from a deeper place.

- Problems lead to opportunities if you look for them.

- Reach out to help another artist (in the broad sense). It's a tough row to hoe, for most of us.

- Repetitive dreams convey a special message.

- Re-reading your favorite books can lead to deeper insight.

- Say what you truly want to say, even if it will leave you open to criticism.

- Seek justice for yourself AND others.

- Self-segregation leads only to stagnation.

- "Simplicity plus depth" is a good goal to strive for.

- Sometimes focus on detail, other times the broad panorama.

- Sometimes I think I learn more from my enemies than my friends about how NOT to behave in this world.

- Speaking truth to power is sometimes met with silence, and that's the most painful truth of all.

- Stay grounded in the reality of where you are, but don't give up on your dreams.

- Stay true to yourself.

- Stop looking at the scoreboard. It just distracts you from playing your best game.

- Stop talking so much and practice listening.

A Thought Experiment

When visiting Tacoma Park, Maryland, I found that I needed to adjust to the culture, where many people spoke Spanish, where no spoken English was heard. In a way, it felt something like adjusting to homelessness, so I wrote this imaginative exercise.

You can experience culture shock, stuck in a motel for a few days, till your money runs out. You can feel paralyzed for a while, afraid to go out ... but the face on TV is generally phony and superficial. After a while you do step out the door and if you have your wits and adaptive skills about you, you realize that you do need some exercise so you walk downtown. At first, you are afraid, but most everyone is polite and nonthreatening. You still have a little money so you go to a fast food restaurant and order from the menu. Then you walk down one of the main streets, just exploring, not thinking about where you might end up in a few days. If you project too much, you may find yourself paralyzed again.

You find a barber who gives a cheap haircut. It's not cool to let your appearance deteriorate too much. You stay aware of your immediate surroundings to avoid any mugging. If you happen to be a writer, you bring a pad and pen with you to write. You may fall into old patterns like talking on the street, even though you are now taking mental medicine. You realize now that you can negotiate your immediate surroundings on foot. There will be muggers in any city though; you must be aware. You come across a sign for a program that might be for the homeless. You head back to the motel to look up homeless resources. And you forget your loneliness for now.

(post-homelessness)

Old Hopes, Old Dreams,

distant pathways,
love is not always what it seems.

Old shoes, torn and tattered by the rain and wind. Old Falcon, barely running, motor knocking, still a thousand miles to go to get back to the South. Memories eat away at me, but that world I'm leaving is already dead and gone.

Old hopes, old dreams, distant pathways,
love is not always what it seems.

Well, keep on driving till dusk turns into night. Check into Motel 6. Sitting up, watching sitcoms. It's a long way from Mary Tyler Moore to where you ended up.

Old hopes, old dreams distant pathways,
love is not always what it seems.

These are the words I wrote in my journal on a distant highway somewhere in Kentucky.

May old hopes and dreams -- somehow,
may they –somehow, be renewed.

(post-homelessness)

Having Gone from Sleeping
in the Parking Lot

of an interstate truck stop, to living in a few homeless shelters, to inhabiting a single room, spring has finally touched me in Northampton.

At dawn, when I walk to the coffee shop alone, there is a kind of luminosity in the air, a deep glow, a hint of tremulousness in new leaves and dark branches. I have been up all night cleaning my cramped living space and discarding many things.

I have been clearing a space in my single room, and in my heart.

(post-homelessness)

Stranded in a Café

Stranded in a café in New England.
Seeking shelter in a Southern kind of town.

Stranded in a blizzard
but it really doesn't matter.
In the spirit you have heard from one you love.

Somewhere in the mountains.
You are stranded in the mountains.

Sheltered from the ruthless and the blind.
Stranded in a blizzard
But it really doesn't matter.
She is trusting and forgiving, she is kind.

A lonely café beckons
Upon the Mohawk Trail.
Just 16 miles from Greenville
Through snow and sleep and hail.

It's light will shine forever
For the desperate and the lost.
Who blithely courted danger
And now must pay the cost.

There are many kinds of faces
In the shelter of a café.
Weather-beaten people

Who have stolen, dreamed and cried.

Many kinds of failures
But it really doesn't matter.
Strangers are protected
By the weather-beaten people
Who have stumbled and survived.

Down This Road

Lonely and scared, wandering the street,
Dressed in baggy pants,
Tattered shoes upon my feet
Scared to talk with strangers,
Or the evil I may meet.
(This ain't the first time) I've been down this road,
Down this road before.

Dreaming of a beauty,
Southern beauty far away,
Hoping for a miracle,
In this city colored gray.
Willing to lose everything,
The price that I must pay.
I've been down this road, Down this road before.

Driven to a shelter,
There's no place else to stay,
Trying to enjoy these,
Tattered grips upon my tray.
Cornered by a minister,
Who tries to teach me to pray,
(This ain't the first time) I've been down this road,
Down this road before.

Trying to resurrect the world,
That I surely knew,

The wind upon my face
Beside the ocean streaked with blue.
Trying to regain some peace,
My world is so askew.
(This ain't the first time) I've been down this road,
Down this road before.

This song is about Joe, a friend I made at the homeless shelter, and his potential to help others in our community ...

The Ballad of Joe Malone and Me

When Joe Malone rides out one night
exploring destiny,
Will fate demand he sell his pride
or share his love for free?

His father drank himself to death
somewhere in Albany.
Did fate demand he binge alone,
then die in misery?

His mother shut the door on him
when he was twenty-three.
Did fate demand she hide her face,
prolong his agony?

Will someone liberate the son
or throw away the key?
Will fate demand he stay confined
or soar into infinity?

Will Joe soon pawn his sweet guitar
along with mystery?
Will fate demand he dumpster dive
and sacrifice his dignity?

The dealers snare the desperate poor,
the folks like Joe and me.
Will fate demand we sell their coke
or save integrity?

You know, homelessness is no fun game
that's played with ecstasy.
A shelter is not filled with love,
it's just an agency.

Now don't pretend it cares for you.
It serves you bitter tea.
A shelter is a place to sleep
for folks like Joe and me?

When Joe Malone rides out one night
exploring destiny,
Will fate demand he sell his soul
or rescue you and me?

When Joe Malone rides out one night
exploring destiny,
Will fate demand he stay confined
or rise into infinity?

When the Homeless Attempt to Help Each Other: A Man Named Ken

In the overnight shelter in Northampton, I met a man named Ken. He was tall, maybe in his fifties, sporting a mustache. Ken was a medic in Vietnam, also a heroin addict, but a caring individual. People were drawn to him, and he was a leader of sorts in the homeless community.

He took me under his wing, to some extent — showed me how to keep my feet dry in winter. Well, it worked for a bit. I remember that he had a girlfriend named Elizabeth, who lived in a tent beside the railroad tracks. She did not like staying in the shelter, maybe because too many of the men would hit on her. I remember she was religious and frequently carried a Bible around with her.

Ken told me a story about a traumatic event that he had in 'nam. He said that a Viet Cong woman, using her baby as a shield, approached him with a rifle. Ken knew that it was him or her – he chose to shoot through the baby to save himself. He never forgave himself for that.

Posted at the shelter was a waiting list for the homeless halfway house. Ken's name was right above mine, and I remember that he allowed me to bump myself past him on the list. I always felt guilty about that, because I made it to the halfway house a couple of months before he did.

Later on, while the halfway house was holding its weekly community meeting downstairs, Ken died of a drug overdose while sitting on the toilet upstairs. I imagined that if he had gotten into the shelter before me, maybe it would have made some kind of difference in terms of his fate. I know that sounds crazy, but that's how I was thinking. The fact that I was the one who found him sitting on the toilet with the needle poised in his left hand accentuated this feeling of guilt, somehow.

Earlier that evening, he asked to speak to me downstairs, but I was too preoccupied to take the time. If he had spoken to me about how he was feeling, I imagine I might have helped him in some way.

During another weekly community meeting at the halfway house, we discussed his death, but I felt — rightly or wrongly — it was perfunctory and more aimed at covering themselves than dealing with the feelings of residents. I thought that staff should have determined Ken's whereabouts on the night he died of an overdose, before proceeding.

This song was written about that incident, as an attempt to heal myself and to commemorate Ken.

Be a True Friend - If You Dare

Well, I want to tell you folks a story
About a man I met one day,
In a shelter in Northampton,
Massachusetts, USA.

He had a gentle, simple manner,
But he lived a hard and crazy life,
He never saw his son in Wooster
And I don't think he had a wife.

He helped me get acquainted
With the danger of the street,
To walk about in winter
While avoiding frozen feet.

I knew he had a problem,
He stuck a needle in his arm,
I knew he could be shady,
But he never did me harm.

The man I'm telling you about
Was a medic in Vietnam,
He could not leave his pain behind,
And yes, he gave a damn.

Before I had a chance to tell him
Just how much I really cared,
I found him overdosed one day,
My gift to him went unshared.

I wish I had had the courage to
Reach out to him back then,
I would have tried to get him help
With the battle he could not win.

Sometimes in life we all need help
And someone to be there.
Be that someone who will reach out,
A true friend, if you dare.